Heavenly Bodies, Earthly Minds

By: Dijon Noble

This book is consecrated to the noble ones of the Earth, past, present and future generations.

This Book may not be reproduced, transmitted, or stored in whole or in part by any means, including graphic, electronic or mechanical without the express written consent of the author except in the case of brief quotations embodied articles and reviews.

ISBN 978-0-615-51302-7

Cover art: "To the womb once more"
By: Dijon Noble

With editorial contributions by Latonda L. Noble

Contents

If I can uplift the mind and spirit of one individual through this manuscript the time and effort I spent in making it will have been well worth it. This collection is simply my thoughts and feelings manifest on paper for the sake of my own mental and spiritual wellbeing as writing down my deeper thoughts and feelings and reflecting upon them, to me is very therapeutic.

I hope that other like-minded individuals will read my humble expressions on various subjects and gain something of benefit. I feel in my view of (God) or the source of life and existence that we can only see (god) through (god's) creation by observing animals and various environments and all things natural we get an insight into the mind of the creator and designer of these things.

I being a creation of the creator of the natural universe, if not anything else I'm a creator and designer myself and thus without ever meeting me these writings will give an insight into my life on this Earth. The Heavens contain everything and without it what would there be?

I

The Heavens and Earth are the works of one maker and by closely observing the nature of both we see that they are one and the same, just as we see that the Earth came from the Heavens and is composed of the same elements, we see that humans and animals both come from the Earth and are composed of the same elements namely fire, water, air, and earth or dense matter.

We are a part of the Earth but equally a part of the Heavens just as a man or woman is a part of their mother, they are equally a part of their grandmother, and just as when a child is developing in the womb of its mother all of the needs of the embryo are supplied by the mother.

All of the nourishing qualities necessary to sustain and provide growth to the unborn child are inherent in its habitat (the womb) and when it emerges it is further provided by its mother in the form of milk, such is nature applied to all the children of the Earth.

II

All needs are fulfilled in the natural environment, food, shelter, clothing, water and most importantly love or synthesis, indeed we are our environment, just as the child is the mother. When you observe nature you can't help but observe the love/synthesis inherent in all things.

The Sun rises every day and provides the light which insures the continuance of all life on Earth, and reflects upon the Moon to provide guidance in the night and the Moon regulates the tides which in turn regulate aquatic life. We observe Birds forming lifelong bonds and protecting each other; replicating themselves and nurturing their young until they are able to fly, feed themselves, and repeat the same process of procreation.

You see the trees provide shelter and food for animals, you see even insects such as Ants and Bees collaborate amongst themselves for the sake of the colony as a whole, and raise they're young until they've become fully developed.

III

We witness these same or similar instances in all species upon the Earth from the largest life forms, (Whales, Elephants, etc.) to the most minute (Gnats, Ants, etc.).

In life what makes these species come together according to the same method by which they came upon this Earth, namely that a male and a female of the same species come together for the advancement of themselves and the species as a whole, procreate and raise their progeny, what is the will that causes this to happen, if it is instinct then what is the source of it?

We see the same "instinct" at work amongst humans in the same forms, just as a female Peacock seeks to procreate with the mate that has the most brilliant color patterns and therefore is the most developed & healthy, or the female Elk who seeks to mate with the male they feel has the qualities which are most conducive to the continuance of life for their species, such as strength to protect their herd.

IV

All species inherently seek mates which have qualities they want their progeny to inherent, by this we come to self-realization through our mates, we seek to manifest our physical ideals through them by wanting to be with a counterpart who is aesthetically pleasing, whose characteristics we admire and instinctually we want our progeny to possess those same traits.

Also to manifest the ideals of our spirit through them, by seeking love, companionship, someone to confide in and share our likes, dislikes, etc. in other words synthesis, by thinking deeply about this we find that we seek to realize the mystery of life, and thus life's maker through our mates.

The maker of life's most prominent attribute is the creation of life, and only through our mates can we realize that attribute within and outside of ourselves, and thereby intimately know our creator, and be an active participant in the fulfillment of the will of that creator.

V

As we see that all natural life seeks to reproduce and replenish itself, so it is with the nature of the Heavens with countless self-replicating bodies consisting of meteors, comets, planets, stars, solar systems, galaxies etc.

 As well as the Earth which nourishes countless species and environment's, humans, animals, marshes, deserts, grasslands, the oceans, continents, etc. We see that by natural law all things replicate through synthesis which can only be described as something like love, and we find that all these things originated with the maker of life and are now inherent in our bodies and minds.

 Thus we come to the realization of the nature of self, that we manifest Heavenly and Earthly divine natural law through our minds and bodies, so may we gain insight into the synthesis of Heavenly Bodies and Earthly Minds.

VI

1
Evening Starlight

She who is the nectar of the flower of innocence imbued with the regenerative scent of women, but a cold wind from a short distance brought decay with swiftness.

Lush things grow decrepit but eyes tend to turn away from signs that show lessons, sweet things in the past will cause bitter times for the whole of mankind, his ideals have changed but the mind of mankind has remained the same.

Consider how beauty that enters the eye may bring ugly thoughts to the mind, frustration is the worse impulse oppressive to some, until it compels itself to be acted upon.

A growing woman is like a flower having diverse directions but without the light of the Sun it cannot move, and is at the mercy of parasites with intent to consume.

What is the worth of infertile soil something that sees itself as worthless has no meaningful purpose, so she became broken extensively and has died on the inside but altogether remains lovely on the surface.

Ah, sigh

In my thought I picture you with me, and my intent brought you within close proximity. To look at you causes longing and the will to freely hear of the pain you are holding, although your laughter causes tranquility to be brought before me.

I may revivify your mind's eye through a words pronouncement, your eyes hold within them love for me in contrast to your heartless actions, but my attachment to you is fertile like soil and unconditioned, but what you bring to me instead of growth is the stress of your accumulated experiences.

Open your emotions to me and may the release of your tears bring you within reach of relief, you are like arid land which through lack of care became desolate, so how I longed for rain to come giving of life alleviating the pain life has brung.

3

Always on my way

I seek refuge in the next day while escaping the last;
I grew bitter with the present while recollecting the
sweetness of the past.

Hope in the midst of struggle is the bright star which
lights my path in this bleak night, it alighted upon
my heart and mind so distant in my vision but still
contained within my sight.

The essence that gave me my breath may provide the
essence that will extinguish my longing, but by my
life the heat and warmth of longing has caused the
biting cold of frustration brought by wanting.

My hope has been longing interspersed with grief, I
was awoken by an eastern breeze and prepare for my
rest westwardly in hopes that by my eyes constant
closure I may find the essence I seek.

Birth and renewal

The womb that brought her forth gave birth to my attachment to her,

A cold night may give birth to a warm day,

But brighter and more rarely seen is a woman of virtue relieved of unclean ways.

In my path many flowers I have picked, inhaled of their various scents and have since considered insufficient.

Worthless is the soil of unfertile ground, but the raised land is beloved by me accentuating the Sun's rays as it wanes in its round.

Many were the days when comfort eluded those without crop, but one cannot cultivate when the fertile embrace of love has escaped.

5

Blinded by darkness

A man may seek throughout life but fail to find contentedness; by night's brightness and day's darkness would it clarify the differences.

Because past instances gave birth to present memories, pleasant times that pass tend to pave the path for misery.

My expectations of life placed a cloak on my sight until circumstances became apparent, and consequently stripped the hope from my awareness.

Speak with me because the warmth of my words provide to a cold heart comfort, but only those who closely listened obtained the benefit while I could not find that my words held self-worth.

Buried in the womb

Let our lifespans be lengthened as we strengthen our capabilities to contain life giving lessons, in acknowledgment of my ascendants may their memory endure like heavenly bodies and when their child returns to eternity may my descendants acknowledge my memory.

This life is sacred but most approach it with irreverence, certainty in their safety and upturned faces, but with humility I hold contempt for this worlds reality, I lie to it although my heart is imbued with honesty and I committed wrongdoing knowing it would never forgive me.

Because the one who gave birth to me has been snatched from me traumatically, my mother I have nowhere to go other than your own household, you have nurtured and sustained many ungrateful children who are on a path leading to nonexistence based on how they are bringing you close to deaths threshold. I pray for stability as I walk the path of every living being on the earth before me, to decompose and disintegrate and become eventually the air that future generations breathe.

I cannot confirm the existence of an earthly heaven but I know what you contained within you was more lasting and precious. If I had the worlds riches I would trade it for the wealth of experience, and the footprint of my experience is supported by your existence every step upon you is in prayer, I will leave my body with you and show you in truth that I too care.

7

Empty everything, fulfill nothing

I put forth a question half complete in hopes that you fulfill the void with eloquent speech, if I requested happiness and peace will you willingly yield yourself to me.

The mark of character lies in the completion of intention, as my words express the intention to complete you will you stand to listen.

By my imagination and inquisitiveness I cannot fathom the stark contrast of excess in content and the void of empty space.

The void of love and fulfillment in your life only became apparent through the expression of emptiness in your eyes in contrast to the beauty of your face.

For my reflection

I praise god for the beauty you possess exchange words with me so I may thank god for your intellect, and cling to my company so that I may avoid a heavy burden between my back and chest.

I feel your absence it's like the lack of warmth for flesh, and who would go unclothed in the cold when they have the option of garments, so may your covering be my presence and your heart my compartment.

When I sense your presence I strain my neck, from darkened clouds the clear rains collect I realize in retrospect, and my feelings were as shallow ponds and clearly in my actions did they reflect.

With dignity I shed tears at present for the sake of tomorrow, uncertain about my loved ones, knowing you as my loved one not knowing if or when you may go.

9

Found wanting and lost nothing

Woman when we speak I feel in all earnestly fulfilled complete to find what I seek, I opened my mouth and let comfort and security exit from my teeth.

Relief to you was felt when we meet like the shade of trees obtained from the threat of desert heat or one suffering from thirst to see a spring leak when death is near and life lies at its brink.

My defeat would be in not providing you with happiness and peace, if harmony between us is not achieved we may as well desist because life is brief between the time when one is conceived and eventually pronounced deceased.

Possibly I will bring you within heights lofty reach and hold your burden up from beneath, so express to me is there a place within you guarded and empty for me to fulfill with contents composed by divinity?

Gazing intently upward

Existence of night and day lies behind my eyes, I drew breath in my perception of the world and exhaled in the essence of time.

In the imprint of my footprint lie's experience, ahead of me stands the unseen, the path of life slowly descends upon me and lays comfortably beneath my feet.

I recognized death through life's reflection and saw neither is my constant companion nor my continual adversary.

My face shone with divinity giving light to what I see, my heart reflected understanding giving wisdom to my mode of speech.

11
Holy day, wholesome night

I grow tired of life but cannot attain rest in the thought of death, because life is a paradigm and death causes perplexion, I seen clearly the transparency of reality but could not obtain its reflection.

The linear time I perceive has passed along without me as I experienced it as an instant, my fortune I read with supreme accuracy as my life occurs in cycles, just as the moons radiance systematically dims and then becomes replenished.

Nights rotate and circumstances change like a books page, experience yields gifts the likes of which transfix eyes already glazed and bestow upon the unlearned the wisdom of a sage.

I strain my neck trying to find where time went and realized moments I thought I owned were my privilege to live, death succeeds life much like day proceeds night, because time is an elusive thing so much so no one can see it, and everyone regrets to appreciate it until it is desperately needed.

I see myself

It is best to encircle yourself with a minute group in your company, and expect truth and loyalty than to be amongst a multitude and be subject to deceit and dishonesty.

The maker made us of the same mold so let it be that we come to know each other, brothers and sisters our father forgave us although we depreciated our mother, time claims us as offspring take the place of parents, we grope through life as if blind although reality is readily apparent.

You seen that from the darkness a child proceeds and when exposed to light it cries and screams, so is our own nature against us or is the world in which we live against our natural interest?

13
I stand vindicated

Night and day contained in my heart and brain
by its alternation my life is sustained, I came to
realize what passed me in this life pass like day
pass into night, what I longed for denied me, by
truth I was tried as illusion tried me.

I was conditioned by my life's experiences
which denied the essential nature of my being;
the temporal things I pursued withdrew from me
and denied my essence, just as summer rain
denies the embrace of the desert, just as the
sun's rays denies a cold day.

And by my life and its essence, through an
inborn sense of shame and nobility, I escaped
the company of the blameworthy and
apologized to myself, and with that made
amends with my own worst enemy.

In need of assistance

Whether to lie down in dignity or walk in disgrace, what man has in life been completely pleased with the path their experiences have paved?

The things that occur clearly show the superior status of the soul in comparison to the mind, because physical experience becomes vague memories irretrievable with the passing of time.

Soul is of the universal womb giving birth to thought, raising up emotions, and manifesting actions, a person may grieve to death for what they have done in life but never would they be able to retract it.

I came into physical existence without the ability to care for myself; I live life wishing I'll have the privilege in death to cry for help.

14

15

Just one of many

What distinguishes those that lived before me,
because an ornate and extravagant casket only
contains a tragedy, a person lives briefly in regards to
eternity, yesterday we were unthought–of, in the
moment we exist, and tomorrow we are always
unsure of. So if you know fulfillment of life you also
know life's commencement, these words of truth
and substance make me wonder if my life is relevant
and purposeful, but would these words have come to
others attention if I was nonexistent and unknown?

Left me with no peace

Your essence is the part of you that intrigues me.

*I would feel more close to death without your presence,
than if my breath attempted to escape my chest.*

*And from your absence I'm left with a greater sense of
bereavement.*

*Your memory leaves a greater imprint on my mind than
what occurs through the passing of time.*

Time has passed but your essence has not passed my mind.

17

Living water

The day was my sight and brought the cover from deceit, consoling me in the light of reality it brought me from the solace I found in sleep.

How sublime it is to see the reflection of magnificence, my soul reached my throat and water was sent, my thirst ascended my hope and stagnant water sullied my essence.

As precipitation fell through eyes which are the windows of the house of life, we laugh and cry sounds pronounced through the fountain of the perceptive mind.

Minds concern for heart

For my beloved I felt the worst, and thought that pleasant thoughts could alleviate painful circumstances and make good for the pain caused at birth.

In the time I've existed in this world I sense problems predominate, so through the alternation of days I strive to find us a safe and secure place.

I've gathered my belongings and in humility asked the heart to be my receptacle, I cried tears for my beloved and bore the burden placed on us both.

18

19

My imagination in person

In all earnestness I could not grasp the light
of your essence, when magnificence hit's the
eye it brings cause for reflection.

Like sunlight giving nourishment to
vegetation your form and face gave
sustenance to my minds notice.

Your words brought solace to a heart that
goes unheard, reverberating goodness
fulfilling the purpose emotions serve.

My mind has attained comfort at the thought
of lucidity, but as of now that I see clearly
my dedication to you became exposed as my
enemy.

My woman in all places

These words sprung forth as the salvation of my soul when in your presence my dwelling is heaven in your absence hell becomes my abode, your love is my lord and the devil in all this boundlessness has no place to exist.

In my heart and mind this experience cannot be referenced, but strangely I know I was a part of your heart and soul in a previous existence, in earnest my love for you is pure worship the reflection of your appearance likens to the depths of the ocean to look at you soothes me I'm calmed by flowing currents.

The spirit of my essence moved upon your bodies surface, that I may immerse myself in your higher self, from what emerged from my lips sprung fertile thoughts to your brain pouring water from betwixt your knees and hips may I drown in your rain.

If I die by that I myself gladly accept death, but you are also my air and the reality of death is to be left breathless, your image clings to my consciousness like a loving kiss clings to lonely lips, I'm at the right hand of god forever her servant.

Lush things grow decrepit

Woman you have a beautiful face but your substance is nothing the void you try to fulfill will reduce you to the lowliest rank, in appearance you are blessed but what you value in excess every woman possess, so why what you value you give away without consideration and thought. So what is greater in worth a woman who can be obtained by a cost or one who through her pains in birth brings forth like rain to the earth, precious water into the barren desert redirect death and quenches life's thirst?

I say according to what I see when youthful and animate lovely is your appearance it caught the attention of the inconsiderate and upon the sensuous it made a heavy imprint, but with decay and whatsoever comes after it you have gained nothing at all in terms of benefit from the life that vanity authored.

I feel sorry for a woman who roams around unguided and cries out aloud like a harlot, and later in age finds herself as an empty page defiled and discarded. And justly I feel sorry for the daughter of an unchaste father desire led him and his progeny followed blindly like a lamb to be slaughtered, to be sacrificed for the temporal things of this life, with random individuals she chose to freely share the outcome was that her natural beauty became a fulfillment of the absence of theirs.

I prefer fertility like I prefer sunlight above storm clouds but pleasant warmth can grow to heat that is violent and thunder will begin to fade after having grown loud. My perception changed and by result of shame I grieve like a motherless child, I change by seeing modesty uncovered, and in the process how a woman would defile the gift which would have made them an honored mother. The inside of her imbued with the warmth of life has become undesirable to me like suffocating cold in windswept nights.

Perennial Love

In this course of life I hope to find one who gives love
freely as does the rays of the sun emanating life giving
light, and could she be held aloft and provide radiance
like a moonlit night. I was a witness to magnificence
and I recognized its worth, a gift from the sky who
cultivated virtue since birth and carved from the
womb was a living likeness of the fertile earth, who
possesses a modest smile and sublime gaze, too pure
and gentle by night and by day to be altered or
changed by the worlds unclean ways.

23
Right by me

Besides our lives what may we share let us divide the spoils of our worldly affairs, from one came pairs from two we all proceed.

I descended from one who from nothing everything comes, the legacy of existence divided between daughters and sons.

My other half to complete you is sacred to me, so accept me like the soil accepts the seed.

Gestate my essential essence and through this bring forth to us a mutual attachment, we are one soul in two bodies may we strive for enhancement.

See me roaming

The journey one takes does satiate the need for a goal, just as heat is not appreciated until one is relieved of the cold.

When crumbs are amassed by the well fed, that is cause for ravenous tears to be shed, but through crying eyes can thirst be retained, and by what they consume can a corpse's life be revived and sustained?

Let me engage every aspect of my senses and consider in bewilderment, if all we knew as reality ceased what would be existent.

I see in depth and consider does this situation cause pain or does pain mold my situation, cries resonate through my ears and because I sense grief has appeared I now seek to hear laughter.

In hopes that a burden may be relieved from my soul, I have undertaken a journey in search of a goal.

25

Talking myself to sleep

On a day by day basis I'm surrounded by fabrications, so I say sincerely your honesty is lovely to me, more valuable than any money and providing my heart with the wealth that is peace.

So please ask that I may give freely reality is not far from a wish simply open your eyes and witness me, reality is not far from a wish and to fulfill your wish gave a shallow heart deep happiness.

Appreciate the ways instilled in me, for my words bring comforting horizons within reach, I know my speech soothes and urges one to sleep but don't close your eyes upon me.

The cycle continues

When one cannot attain the object he covets he should then covet his attainments, gently I walked a path trodden by the aimless and could not conduct myself in any way other than abasement.

What I seek continually flees from me, yet the thought of it became my constant companion and eventually my adversary, and until the burden on my back and chest and what beats in between is relieved I pray I may not seek that which is fleeting.

The alternation of days brought me further away from a meaningful objective; I became a subject of my own inclination a continuation without direction.

26

27

Those that left before me

When I have died my dearest apologies extend to those who felt sorry for me, so out of pity sing and dance over me because I have transitioned to an existence free from enmity, I'm living when grief and pain no longer worry my being, may I radiate happiness while my relatives rejoice in my company.

We have earthly bodies and heavenly minds, my consciousness transcended the perimeters of my mind when my body becomes buried through the weariness of time, may my breath flow through the blood of my descendants.

To those that love me I ask for no thanks for the good I gave and for my mistakes I ask for forgiveness, my ancestors shined light upon me and I'm a reflection of the past, I seen through eyes already closed and by feeling became guided in my path.

Up from the ground

How the root gives purpose to the plant which it comforts with stability, the root with likeness to my soul holding my form up from beneath, in turn the world may behold the blooming that's made visible by the essence of life's fertility.

I revert to my root when life becomes cold and my reserves of energy grow empty, and ascend from my origin when life's light shines upon what I see.

The root and the earth that encompasses it are indeed inseparable entities, the supreme source of existence and the soul which sprung forth from it as a miniscule component can be seen as the soil and root of my being in its totality.

So behold how the plant is the likeness of me as the eye perceives, now I convey the abundance of source, matter, and spirit in hopes that the root of the seedling may become uplifted.

When I know now

If I know fulfillment of desire with no substance, afterward I know destruction, I recognized reality when my eyesight malfunctioned, because illusion tempted me dulled my senses and lessened my proficiency.

I arrayed myself in luminous garments, extended gentility and covered my harshness, I walk aright either in prosperity or hardship, I questioned with truth those who knew and sincerely hope the above words be proven as true.

If I know truth gratitude follows, I see my ends and mean to bring good for tomorrow, yesterday I was unthought-of, today I relinquish my environments product.

When water breaks

One cannot tell the depth of the sea by studying its surface, when I began to see life my eye sight lost all outward purpose.

If I found what I seek I fear it may leave me quickly, just as in death the breath leaves the body.

I'm dependent upon a collective mass of flesh within the structure of my chest which bears down on me often.

When each one of us becomes deceased we pray the essence of our memory will provide our descendants with peace.

Whatever proceeds from the womb is deposited in the depths of darkness; from the darkness of the womb I emerged to see the light of hardship.

30

31
Wise counsel

Be close to me as a bird is to its wings, study the
earth and observe how the herb is dependent
upon the seed. The provisions I provide cannot
be measured in material acquisitions, but it exalts
your status above that of kings and queens it
brings direction to the majestic. You hear me and
in your heart entered indescribable longing
compelling you to bring me nearer, you have
been inspired by your sight and sustained by the
guidance I've placed between your ears, with that
invest deep thought, I gave you a gift that cannot
be obtained at a cost.

With sincerity

In thanks to the incomparable, the hidden source of all existence, who molded the sun and moon and made them regulate the living and dead.

The most generous who's provision composed of moist and dry, heat and cold, brought taste to the tongue and created the stars encompassing the earth, with likeness to the limitless mind, in the minute confines of men and women's heads.

Creation embraces me after I'm extracted from the unseen, my consciousness reached the limits of the inaccessible, I honor and welcome myself in thanks to the incomparable.

32

33

Woman above

My woman in all places, cling yourself to me and accept a life of austerity, you have seen bodies heavenly but could not define its shimmering, in much the same way you could not contain my simile.

I wish I could raise you like light raises the morning, but the moon has declined and took with it my spirit, I would relinquish emptiness and hold you with earnest, but I'm not allowed and like the sun which wanes in its round from adulthood to child my light has diminished, I would never attain your equal but I will obtain my life's commencement.

But I ask myself who else could be worthy to obtain you, I doubt they can provide you with pleasure from the pain that I go through, a portion comes from not having you and it does not subside, your absence so much affected my mind I almost prayed for my own demise, to fulfill the space in my heart you left would take boundless time.

Like the universal mother who placed her child on the river of stars surface, maybe you will return to me ahead of eternity on the back of flowing currents.

www.ingramcontent.com/pod-product-compliance
Lightning Source LLC
LaVergne TN
LVHW091211080426
835509LV00006B/942